The Wayfinders

A 10-Week Faith Journey for Students

Small Group Facilitator's Guide

Equipping young people to hear God's voice, walk in freedom, and influence their world for Jesus.

Rebecca Harp

Unless otherwise noted, Scriptures are paraphrased from New International Version (NIV) or New Living Translation (NLT).

ISBN: 979-8-9959160-0-0

We are God's masterpiece. He made us new
in Christ Jesus, so we can do the good things
he planned for us long ago.

Ephesians 2:10

CONTENTS

A Note for Facilitators

Thank you for stepping up to lead and guide small groups of young people and future leaders. Your yes is changing the world one person at a time.

Before each session, spend some time with the Lord. Pray through the content, test it out for yourself if it feels new, and ask Holy Spirit to guide your teaching and be at work in and through you. He will!

Each week is designed for a 45–60 minute session. The layout for each week typically follows a similar rhythm:

- ☑ Opening Prayer (1 min)
- ☑ Group Connect & Activation Check-In (5–8 min)
- ☑ Previous Week Review / Laughing at Lies (5–8 min)
- ☑ Main Teaching with Scripture (15-20 min)
- ☑ Group Discussion Prompts (10 min)
- ☑ Activation (8 min)
- ☑ Assignments for Next Week (5 min)

Closing Prayer is not identified each week, but it can be implemented to review and bless what students have coming up in the week ahead. It's also an opportunity to activate students to pray over each other.

Helpful Supplies Each Week

Student Companion Guide (sold separately), journals, writing utensils, whiteboard with dry-erase markers (helpful, not necessary).

GETTING STARTED

ACTIVATION: **Facilitator Prayer**

"Holy Spirit, what would you like to do during this small group?"

Week 1

Identity: *Who Do You Say I Am?*

OPENING

Open with a short prayer inviting Holy Spirit to guide your time together.

Group Introductions — Each Student Shares

Name, area of interest

One thing you like about yourself, OR one area where you know you're making progress

One thing you'd like to learn over the next 10 weeks

Note Keep this light and welcoming. The goal is for every person to feel seen and safe as the group gets started.

SCRIPTURAL FOUNDATION

"In the last days, God says, I will pour out my Spirit upon all people. Your sons and daughters will prophesy. ..." **— Acts 2:17 NLT**

"How precious are your thoughts about me, O God. They cannot be numbered! I can't even count them; they outnumber the grains of sand! ..." **— Psalm 139:17–18 NLT**

INTRO TO HOLY SPIRIT + OUR THOUGHTS

1. Who Is Holy Spirit?

Living a Christian life can feel hard or even boring — but that's usually because we're missing Holy Spirit. He is God's Spirit, living inside us, guiding and empowering us to become everything God created us to be. Jesus told His disciples before He left earth: "It is for your good that I am going away. Unless I go, the Advocate will not come to you" (John 16:7). That Advocate is Holy Spirit — and His coming was always part of God's plan for you.

2. Our Thoughts Don't All Come From Us

The thoughts in our minds can come from three places: from us, from God, and from satan — the enemy of our souls. The enemy loves to drop thoughts of "not enough", discouragement, or fear into our minds. But here's the good news: just because a thought shows up doesn't mean you have to think it. You get to choose.

One powerful way to deal with the enemy's lies? Laugh at them. Laughter disempowers the lie and reminds us it has no real authority over us.

Note: The 'Laughing at Lies' exercise recurs weekly. This is intentional. Lies are unhelpful thoughts that can originate from the father of lies, the enemy of our soul, seeking to dissuade us from our heavenly identity and purpose. Repetition builds a new habit of identifying and rejecting lies quickly. Be gentle, never laugh at a person — only at the lie. Can write each lie on the whiteboard as students name them. After each one, laugh together as a group — at the lie, not the person. Then discuss the scriptural truth that replaces it.

["... the devil ... he has always hated the truth, because there is no truth in him. When he lies, it is consistent with his character; for he is a liar and the father of lies." **— John 8:44 NLT**]

GROUP DISCUSSION

💬 What are some common lies or unhelpful thoughts that like to show up in your mind?

💬 How do you currently handle those thoughts — do you push back, or do they tend to stick around?

💬 What does it mean to you that God's thoughts about you outnumber the grains of sand?

HEARING FROM GOD

God loves to communicate with us. His *logos* word is the written scripture. His *rhema* word is His spoken, "right now" communication to us personally. He speaks through thoughts and pictures in our minds, scripture that jumps out at us, the voices of trusted people, dreams and more. Any communication from God will align with His loving nature and will not contradict scripture.

4 Keys to Hearing God's Voice *(credit: Mark Virkler)*:

- *Still yourself* — slow down, quiet your body and thoughts
- *See* — picture Jesus in your mind's eye
- *Spontaneity* — notice the gentle, uplifting thoughts that arise
- *Record* — write down what you receive and evaluate it later against God's character revealed in scripture

ACTIVATION: Get out your journal. Ask God: "Heavenly Father, who do you say I am?" Write down the encouraging, uplifting thoughts that come to mind.

STUDENT ASSIGNMENTS FOR NEXT WEEK

👉 Student 1: Bring an appropriate joke to share (under 1 min)

👉 Student 2: Bring a real story of God's goodness to tell (under 2 min)

👉 Student 3: Bring something encouraging to share with the group (under 2 min)

Note: Student assignments are designed to increase student engagement and leadership. Sharing appropriate humor and laughing together increases connection (Romans 14:17). Talking about God's goodness (testimonies) grows faith and expectation He will do it again (Revelation 19:10). Encouraging words build up others and are a key trait of good leadership (Hebrews 10:24-25). Each of these also gives students an opportunity to practice communication skills.

FACILITATOR NOTES ✨

____

____

____

____

____

____

____

____

____

____

____

____

____

____

Week 2

Friendships: *Who We Surround Ourselves With*

OPENING

Open with prayer. Invite Holy Spirit to come and fill each student afresh.

GROUP CONNECT

How were you a good friend this week? Go around the room and celebrate each other's progress — cheer each other on!

Student Activations (from last week's assignments):

- Student 1: Appropriate Joke (< 1 min)
- Student 2: God story / Testimony (< 2 min)
- Student 3: Encouragement for the Group (< 2 min)

REVIEW: LAUGHING AT LIES

Each student writes a lie that crossed their mind this past week on the whiteboard. As a group, laugh at each one (at the lie, not the person!). Then replace it with a truth.

Facilitator Note: *Remind students: just because a thought comes to mind doesn't mean it's true or that it came from them. We boot those thoughts out. We don't let them set up camp. (And sometimes what presents as a lie or worry is a chance for wise reflection. Example: "You won't do well on your test" is a chance to evaluate if wise study habits have been applied.)*

SCRIPTURAL FOUNDATION

"Walk with the wise and become wise, for a companion of fools suffers harm." **— Proverbs 13:20 NIV**

"And let us consider how we may spur one another on toward love and good deeds, not giving up meeting together... but encouraging one another..." **— Hebrews 10:24–25 NIV**

"And Jesus grew in wisdom and stature, and in favor with God and man." **— Luke 2:52 NIV**

THE POWER OF WHO'S AROUND YOU

The people we surround ourselves with have enormous influence over our thoughts, attitudes, and choices. Our inner circle shapes us, so we want to be intentional about who gets that kind of access. This isn't a reason to treat people poorly who are different from us or who aren't walking with God — it's wisdom about where we invest our closest friendships.

Qualities of a good friend:

- Encourages and builds you up
- Is kind with their words — to you AND to others
- Helps you want to be better
- Has their own hopes and dreams and is going somewhere
- Values faith and time with God

Signs a friendship may be pulling you down:

- Your language or behavior gets worse when you're together
- They tear down others behind their backs
- There's constant drama or chaos

◆ You feel worse about yourself after spending time with them

GROUP DISCUSSION

💬 What is one quality of a good friend that stands out most to you, and why?

💬 Share an example of a time a friend encouraged you or called something good out in you.

💬 Is there one way you could level up as a friend this week — not condemning yourself, just observing and growing?

💡 **ACTIVATION:** Think of one person you can encourage this week. Ask Holy Spirit who it is and what to say — then pay attention to what comes to mind. Do it!

JOURNALING WITH GOD

Journal prompt: "Heavenly Father, what are you celebrating about me from this past week?"

APPLICATION THIS WEEK

Throughout the week, reflect on your closest friendships. What is one step you can take this week to surround yourself with uplifting, God-honoring friendships and influences – and be a positive influence in your current relationships? Are there any friendships or influences you need to hit the pause button on, because they aren't taking you down the right path?

STUDENT ASSIGNMENTS FOR NEXT WEEK

👉 Student 1: Bring a joke (< 1 min)

👉 Student 2: Bring a real God story (< 2 min)

👉 Student 3: Bring something kind or encouraging to share (< 2 min)

FACILITATOR NOTES ✨

Week 3

Inputs: *What We Put In Us Matters*

OPENING

Open with a 1-minute prayer, inviting Holy Spirit.

Group Connect

How were you a good friend this week? Go around the room and celebrate each other's progress — cheer each other on!

Student Activations

- 👉 Student 1: Appropriate Joke (< 1 min)
- 👉 Student 2: God story / Testimony (< 2 min)
- 👉 Student 3: Encouragement for the Group (< 2 min)

REVIEW: LAUGHING AT LIES + JOURNALING

Write a lie from the past week on the whiteboard — laugh at it together.

Then take a few minutes to journal with God: "Heavenly Father, what are you celebrating about me this week?"

SCRIPTURAL FOUNDATION

"Your harvest reflects the seeds you plant. If you live for yourself and worldly desires, you will reap destruction. But if you live by the

Spirit, you will harvest the blessings of eternal life." **— Galatians 6:8**

YOU BECOME WHAT YOU TAKE IN

Everything we take in — the books we read, the shows we watch, the music we listen to, the social media we scroll — matters. We are most likely to reflect what we surround ourselves with. You are training your own mind with every input you choose.

Questions to ask about what you're consuming:

- What is this trying to get me to believe?
- Does this point me toward God or away from Him?
- Does this leave me feeling more hopeful and more like myself — or more afraid and more unlike myself?
- Is this calling out the best in me?

Whatever you spend the most time with will start shaping your thoughts, words, and actions. If you constantly take in negative, unhealthy, or unwise content, it will eventually show up in your attitude, words, and behavior. What is stored up in your mind and heart eventually makes its way out.

It's also worth knowing: books, shows, and music can carry half-truths. Half-truths feel partially right but leave you conflicted. Love with truth and truth with love is the full picture. Love without truth, or truth without love, is only part of the gospel.

The good news? This principle works in a positive way too. When you:

- Spend time in God's Word
- Enjoy His presence

- Fill your mind with things that honor Him

...you start reflecting more of Jesus. Your life, your choices, and even your influence on others will begin to reflect His goodness.

GROUP DISCUSSION

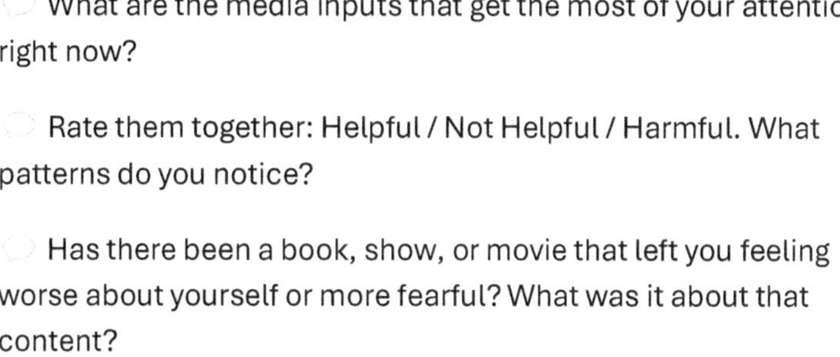

What are the media inputs that get the most of your attention right now?

Rate them together: Helpful / Not Helpful / Harmful. What patterns do you notice?

Has there been a book, show, or movie that left you feeling worse about yourself or more fearful? What was it about that content?

ACTIVATION: This week, before watching a show or starting a book, pause and ask Jesus: 'Is this a good idea for me right now?' Notice whether you feel peace or hesitation. If you feel peace to proceed, then ask: 'Is there anything you want to show me through this?' Pay attention to what comes to mind.

STUDENT ASSIGNMENTS FOR NEXT WEEK

Student 1: Bring a joke (< 1 min)

Student 2: Bring a real God story (< 2 min)

Student 3: Bring something kind or encouraging to share (< 2 min)

Week 4

Favor: *Train Others How to Treat You*

OPENING

Open with a 1-minute prayer, inviting Holy Spirit. Check in — how is everyone doing?

Student Activations

👉 Student 1: Appropriate Joke (< 1 min)

👉 Student 2: God story / Testimony (< 2 min)

👉 Student 3: Encouragement for the Group (< 2 min)

REVIEW: LAUGHING AT LIES — REPLACE IT WITH TRUTH

Write lies on the board. Laugh. Then this week, replace each lie with a scripture truth. Use the examples below or find your own:

◆ *Bad grades* → "Good planning and hard work lead to prosperity." (Prov. 21:5) I plan well and I work hard.

◆ *Not good enough* → "I am confident that He who began a good work in me will complete it." (Phil. 1:6)

◆ *Fear/anxiety* → "God has not given me a spirit of fear but of power, love, and a sound mind." (2 Tim. 1:7)

SCRIPTURAL FOUNDATION

"And Jesus grew in wisdom and stature, and in favor with God and man." **— Luke 2:52 NIV**

YOU TRAIN PEOPLE HOW TO TREAT YOU

In every environment we're in — school, church, sports, family — we are teaching the people around us how to treat us. We do this through our actions, our attitudes, and our words. The choices we make, often the small ones, add up to a reputation. And that reputation either opens doors or closes them.

Practical ways to earn respect and build good relationships:

◆ *Show up on time* — it communicates that you value others and keep your word

◆ *Be gracious, even when it's hard* — how you treat people when it's difficult says everything

◆ *Use encouraging words* — your words shape how others think about you

◆ *Be a problem-solver* — look for ways to add value, not just to receive

When you've messed up:

We all fall short. The good news is, you can always learn from a mistake, apologize and make it right, make small changes, and celebrate your progress. One of the best things about following Jesus is that He is always helping us grow and transform. Every single day.

GROUP DISCUSSION

💭 What's one area where you're already doing well in how you show up for others?

💭 What's one area where you think you could level up — without condemnation, just honest growth?

💭 Can you think of someone you know who carries themselves with a quiet confidence and respect? What do they do that you admire?

Note: Can have students demo good vs. poor body language, eye contact, handshakes, and posture with the group. Have fun with it — exaggerate the bad examples for a laugh, then model the good. Invite students to practice with each other.

💡 ACTIVATION: This week: make your bed every single morning. Why? Small acts of discipline build momentum and send a message to your brain — I follow through. If you already make your bed: add one new habit that would surprise and delight your parents or loved ones. Report back next week!

STUDENT ASSIGNMENTS FOR NEXT WEEK

👉 Student 1: Bring a joke (< 1 min)

👉 Student 2: Bring a real God story (< 2 min)

👉 Student 3: Bring something kind or encouraging to share (< 2 min)

Week 5

The Mechanics: *Salvation & Sanctification*

OPENING

Open with a 1-minute prayer, inviting Holy Spirit.

Student Activations

👉 Student 1: Appropriate Joke (< 1 min)

👉 Student 2: God story / Testimony (< 2 min)

👉 Student 3: Encouragement for the Group (< 2 min)

Note: You can remind students of the why behind the weekly activations: humor connects us. Sharing God stories increases our faith for what God will do again. Encouragement builds courage. These moments also give students a low-stakes opportunity to lead and speak in front of others — that's practice for the rest of their lives.

Activation Check-In

How did the new daily habit go this week? Let each student share briefly — celebrate every win! Claps and cheers work here!

REVIEW

Give students a chance to recap last week's content: Train Others How to Treat You. Include a quick demo from students of posture, eye contact, and handshakes if time allows.

SCRIPTURAL FOUNDATION

"Repent and turn back to God so your sins can be forgiven, and you will experience refreshing from being in His presence, and He will send you Christ Jesus." **— Acts 3:19-20**

"God saved you by his grace when you believed. And you can't take credit for this; it is a gift from God. Salvation is not a reward for the good things we have done, so none of us can boast about it." **— Ephesians 2:8–9 NLT**

"If you openly declare Jesus is Lord and believe in your heart God raised him from the dead, you will be saved. It is by believing in your heart that you are made right with God, and by confessing with your mouth that you are saved." **— Romans 10:9-10**

WHAT IS SIN & REPENTANCE?

Did you know "sin" is actually an archery term? It means "to miss the mark" — like an arrow that doesn't hit the bullseye. Sin happens when we miss God's best for us. It's not about being a bad person. It's about human nature not lining up with God's holy and perfect ways. We all fall short! As our Creator, He knows what's best for us and those around us.

What does it mean to repent?

Repentance is more than saying sorry. It means changing your mind. It looks like:

- ☑ Admitting where we missed the mark — "God, I got this wrong."
- ☑ Asking for forgiveness — "Please forgive me and help me grow."
- ☑ Thanking Jesus for His help — "It's your work in me that makes me better."

The Good News: Salvation

When we choose to believe in Jesus Christ — confessing with our mouths and believing in our hearts — everything changes. His Spirit comes to live in us. We are forgiven. We are in right relationship with our Heavenly Father. We have full access to His love, His guidance, His power, and His promises. This is what salvation means. It's not a reward we earn. It's a gift we receive.

And sanctification? That's the ongoing process of being made more like Jesus over the course of our lives. Every day, He's growing us. That's the life-long adventure we're on.

GROUP DISCUSSION

Has there ever been a time you were carrying something you needed to let go of — a mistake, a grudge, or shame — and you finally gave it to God? What happened?

What is one area of your life you'd love to grow and change? What would it look like to invite Jesus into that specific area?

Has everyone here made a personal decision and confession of faith to follow Jesus? (This is a good moment for the facilitator to invite anyone who hasn't to pray and receive Jesus as Lord and Savior.)

ACTIVATION: Journal: "Jesus, is there anything You want me to repent of right now?" Pause, write what comes. Then follow the three steps: admit, ask forgiveness, thank Him. If you'd like to receive Jesus as your Lord and Savior today, pray: "Jesus, I love You. Would You come live in me? I accept You as my Lord and Savior." *[Salvation is a spiritual event and sanctification is the lifelong process of our natural selves or our souls (mind, will, emotions) catching up to the spiritual reality of salvation.]*

STUDENT ASSIGNMENTS FOR NEXT WEEK

👉 Student 1: Bring a joke (< 1 min)

👉 Student 2: Bring a real God story (< 2 min)

👉 Student 3: Bring something kind or encouraging to share (< 2 min)

FACILITATOR NOTES ✨

____

____

____

____

____

____

____

____

____

____

____

____

____

____

____

____

Week 6

God With Us — Part 1: *Holy Spirit*

OPENING

Open with prayer — invite Holy Spirit to come and fill each student fresh and full.

Student Activations

👉 Student 1: Appropriate Joke (< 1 min)

👉 Student 2: God story / Testimony (< 2 min)

👉 Student 3: Encouragement for the Group (< 2 min)

GROUP CONNECT + JOURNALING

Relational Check-In

Share an example of how you encouraged someone this week, or how you were a good friend. Celebrate each other's progress — cheer each other on!

Journaling

💬 What do you sense God is doing in you right now? What might He be growing or developing in you through your current circumstances?

SCRIPTURAL FOUNDATION

"But very truly I tell you, it is for your good that I am going away. Unless I go away, the Advocate [Holy Spirit] will not come to you; but if I go, I will send him to you." **— John 16:7 NIV**

"... God says, 'I will pour out My Spirit on everyone. Your sons and daughters will prophesy, young people will see visions. ...'" **— Acts 2:17**

WHO IS THE HOLY SPIRIT?

Holy Spirit is not a dove or a character from Pentecost. He is God's Spirit — living inside us when we accept Jesus into our lives — available to guide and empower us for everything we are meant to be, do, and accomplish while we're here on earth. Jesus said it Himself — it was better for us that He went away, because then Holy Spirit could come. That's how important this is.

The Holy Spirit works in two powerful ways:

- He lives inside us when we accept Jesus — comforting, guiding, strengthening, and changing us from the inside out.

- He comes upon us when we ask and partner with Him in faith — giving us insight and power to love and serve others (John 14:12).

When Holy Spirit is at work in and through us, we can:

- Walk in God's wisdom and direction for our lives
- Pray for others with boldness and compassion
- Receive creative, heavenly solutions for real challenges
- Encourage, comfort, and build up the people around us

The power of Holy Spirit always points back to Jesus. And you can always ask for more of Him. He loves to fill and refill His children.

GROUP DISCUSSION

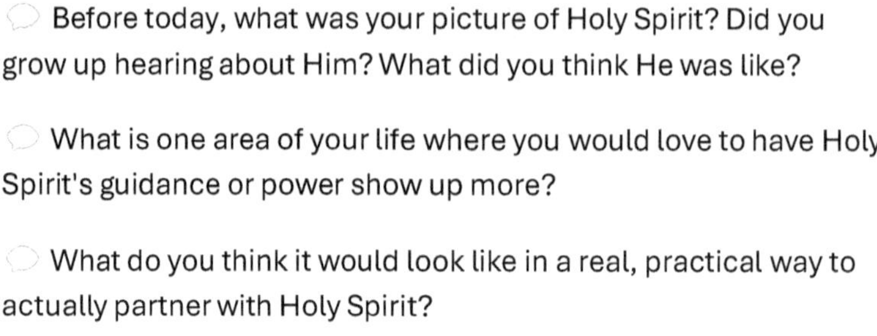

💬 Before today, what was your picture of Holy Spirit? Did you grow up hearing about Him? What did you think He was like?

💬 What is one area of your life where you would love to have Holy Spirit's guidance or power show up more?

💬 What do you think it would look like in a real, practical way to actually partner with Holy Spirit?

💡 **ACTIVATION:** Have you ever invited Holy Spirit to work in your life? Take a moment right now to pray: "Heavenly Father, fill me with Your Holy Spirit. Help me walk in Your power and wisdom today." Then ask: What is one way I can listen for Your guidance this week?

STUDENT ASSIGNMENTS FOR NEXT WEEK

👉 Student 1: Bring a joke (< 1 min)

👉 Student 2: Bring a real God story (< 2 min)

👉 Student 3: Bring something kind or encouraging to share (< 2 min)

FACILITATOR NOTES

Week 7

God With Us — Part 2: *Experiencing God's Presence*

OPENING

Open with a 1-minute prayer, inviting Holy Spirit.

Student Activations

👉 Student 1: Appropriate Joke (< 1 min)

👉 Student 2: God story / Testimony (< 2 min)

👉 Student 3: Encouragement for the Group (< 2 min)

GROUP CONNECT + REVIEW

Check-In

What are you celebrating about yourself from the previous week? Celebrate each other's progress — cheer each other on!

Review Last Week

Holy Spirit works in us (comforting, guiding, sanctifying) and upon us (empowering us for others). The Holy Spirit always points to Jesus. Any questions from last week?

SCRIPTURAL FOUNDATION

"Come close to God, and God will come close to you ..." **— James 4:8 NLT**

"The Lord goes before you and will be with you; he will never leave you or forsake you. Do not be afraid or discouraged." **— Deuteronomy 31:8**

GOD IS ALWAYS WITH YOU

Once you've believed in Jesus and received His Holy Spirit, God's presence is with you — permanently. He is omnipresent, which means He is everywhere, all the time (Jeremiah 23:23–24). You literally cannot hide from Him. And you would never want to.

But even though He is always with us, we can grow in how much we're aware of His presence. Think of it like a friendship. The more intentional time you spend together, the more natural it becomes to notice they're in the room and recognize their communication style with you.

How to grow in awareness of God's presence:

- *Praise Him* — thank Him for who He is
- *Pray* — talk to Him about everything, including the small stuff
- *Worship* — sing to Him, or just sit quietly in awe of His goodness
- *Seek and wait* — read scripture and spend quiet time listening

What can God's presence feel like?

Everyone experiences Him a little differently. It might feel like: a deep, unexpected peace in the middle of chaos. A sudden joy when you least expect it. A warmth or a heaviness. Heat or trembling. No matter how He shows up for you, cherish those moments. They are real. He is near. And know that He is still near, even if you don't feel something.

GROUP DISCUSSION

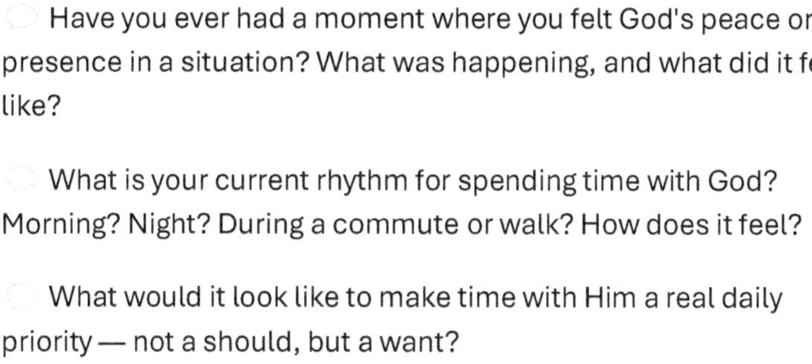

Have you ever had a moment where you felt God's peace or presence in a situation? What was happening, and what did it feel like?

What is your current rhythm for spending time with God? Morning? Night? During a commute or walk? How does it feel?

What would it look like to make time with Him a real daily priority — not a should, but a want?

ACTIVATION: Spend time with Jesus today. Sit somewhere quiet, or play soft worship music. Think about Him — His goodness, what He's done for you. Stay there until you sense His presence. It may feel like peace, warmth, or a settling in your heart. Then just enjoy the moment and time together. This is a Spirit to spirit moment.

JOURNALING PROMPT

"Heavenly Father, what do You want to give me today that I need for what's ahead?" Then ask, "Is there anything you want me to let go of, to give to You, because you are handling it for me?"

STUDENT ASSIGNMENTS FOR NEXT WEEK

Student 1: Bring a joke (< 1 min)

Student 2: Bring a real God story (< 2 min)

👉 Student 3: Bring something kind or encouraging to share (< 2 min)

FACILITATOR NOTES ✨

Week 8

God's Blueprint: *Family, Identity & God's Design*

OPENING

Open with a 1-minute prayer, inviting Holy Spirit.

Group Connect

What progress are you celebrating about yourself? (Go around the room — everyone cheers for each person!)

Student Activations

- Student 1: Appropriate Joke (< 1 min)
- Student 2: God story / Testimony (< 2 min)
- Student 3: Encouragement for the Group (< 2 min)

SCRIPTURAL FOUNDATION

"They know the truth about God because he has made it obvious to them. For ever since the world was created, people have seen the earth and sky. Through everything God made, they can clearly see his invisible qualities—his eternal power and divine nature. So they have no excuse for not knowing God. Yes, they knew God, but they wouldn't worship him as God or even give him thanks. And they began to think up foolish ideas of what God was like. As a result, their minds became dark and confused." — **Romans 1:19–21 NLT**

"I knew you before I formed you in your mother's womb. Before you were born I set you apart ..." — **Jeremiah 1:5 NLT**

GOD'S DESIGN FOR FAMILY & IDENTITY

Cultural issues can feel tricky to navigate. We want to be kind, loving, and compassionate — and those are genuinely good, God-given qualities. But God is also holy, and He has a perfect original design for how we are meant to live and who we are meant to be.

From the beginning of creation:

- God created humans as male and female — each unique, valuable, and designed with specific purpose
- He designed marriage as a covenant between one man and one woman
- Children are a blessing that come from that covenant
- A dad provides identity, protection, and provision; a mom provides comfort, nurture, and teaching

When life doesn't look like the perfect plan:

Not everyone's family situation looks the same — and God sees and deeply cares for every person whose situation is different. If this is your story, you are not alone. God is a loving Heavenly Father who wants to provide everything an earthly father or mother would, and more. He is near to the broken-hearted (Psalm 34:18). His love and purpose for you never change.

Why it matters that God made you:

Many voices in the world want to tell you who you are and who you are not — movies, music, social media, peers, even well-meaning friends and family. But who is better suited to tell you who you are than the one who made you? Your Heavenly Father created you with a specific identity and a specific purpose. The exact mix of you is incredibly valuable.

GROUP DISCUSSION

💭 What is something unique about how God made you — a strength, a personality trait, a passion — that you are starting to appreciate more?

💭 When the world tries to tell you who you are, what messages do you hear most? How do those measure up against what God says?

💭 What is your favorite object at home that you feel like really describes your heart? (A fun, lighter connection question!)

LISTENING PRAYER EXERCISE

Guide students into a quiet moment. Play soft instrumental worship if helpful. Walk them through this:

- Picture Jesus in your mind's eye. He is smiling at you.
- Ask Him: "Jesus, what lie have I been believing about myself?" Write it down. Then picture yourself placing it in His open hand.
- Now ask: "Jesus, who do you say I am?" Write whatever loving, encouraging thoughts come.

💡 **ACTIVATION:** This week: ask God "Who do you say I am?" in your quiet time. Write down what you hear. Let it be bigger and wilder than you'd expect — God's plans for us usually are. Remind yourself this week: I am deeply loved, chosen, and created on purpose, with purpose.

STUDENT ASSIGNMENTS FOR NEXT WEEK

👉 Student 1: Bring a joke (< 1 min)

👉 Student 2: Bring a real God story (< 2 min)

👉 Student 3: Bring something kind or encouraging to share (< 2 min)

FACILITATOR NOTES ✨

Week 9

Forgiveness: *Healing Your Heart*

OPENING

Open with a 1-minute prayer, inviting Holy Spirit.

Group Connect

How did the last week go? What progress are you celebrating about yourself? (After each share, cheer each other on!)

Student Activations

- 👉 Student 1: Appropriate Joke (< 1 min)
- 👉 Student 2: God story / Testimony (< 2 min)
- 👉 Student 3: Encouragement for the Group (< 2 min)

SCRIPTURAL FOUNDATION

"Dear friend, I pray that you stay healthy and that everything goes well for you, just as your soul is thriving." — **3 John 1:2**

"Bear with each other and forgive one another if any of you has a grievance against someone. Forgive as the Lord forgave you." — **Colossians 3:13 NIV**

""Shouldn't you have had mercy on your fellow servant just as I had on you?" ...This is how my heavenly Father will treat each of you unless you forgive your brother or sister from your heart." — **Matthew 18:33, 35 NIV**

THE POWER OF FORGIVENESS

The best way to stay emotionally healthy is to be quick to forgive. Forgiveness doesn't mean what happened was okay. It doesn't mean you're saying the person was right. Forgiveness means you're not going to hold onto it anymore. You're not going to let it take up space in your heart and mind. You're handing it to God to deal with — because He is better at justice than we are.

When someone hurts you, bring it to God:

- *Tell Him what happened* — "God, this really hurt me."
- *Tell Him how you feel* — "I feel frustrated, sad, betrayed."
- *Ask for His wisdom* — "How do you want me to handle this?"

How our family relationships can shape how we see God *(source: ConnectUp)*:

- Hurts from our dad can affect how we view God the Father — our provider, protector, and source of identity (Phillippians 4:19; Psalm 46:1; 1 Peter 2:9)
- Hurts from our mom can affect how we see Holy Spirit — the comforter, nurturer, and teacher (John 14:18; Romans 5:5; John 14:26)
- Hurts from siblings or friends can affect how we relate to Jesus — the one who walks alongside us (Romans 8:29,39)

That's why it's so important to deal with our hurts quickly, and not let them fester. When we process pain with God, we stay close to Him and to the people around us.

Setting Healthy Boundaries:

Forgiveness does not mean unlimited access. Sometimes we need to set healthy boundaries with people who are consistently disrespectful, unkind, or harmful. Boundaries protect us and also communicate to the other person what healthy relationship looks like. You can forgive someone and still have a boundary with them.

GROUP DISCUSSION

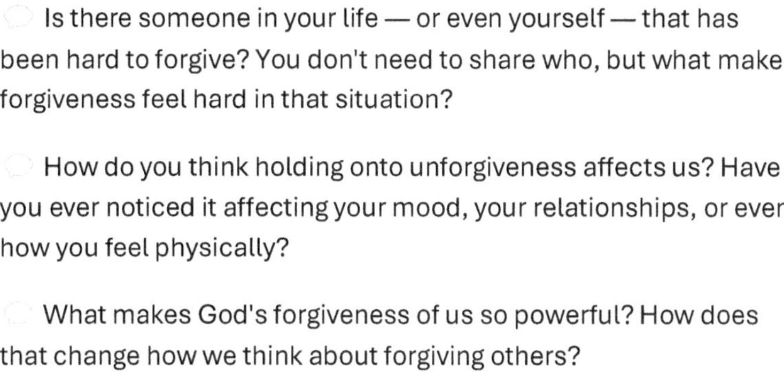

Is there someone in your life — or even yourself — that has been hard to forgive? You don't need to share who, but what makes forgiveness feel hard in that situation?

How do you think holding onto unforgiveness affects us? Have you ever noticed it affecting your mood, your relationships, or even how you feel physically?

What makes God's forgiveness of us so powerful? How does that change how we think about forgiving others?

ACTIVATION: Picture in your mind how much Jesus loves you. Now picture how much He loves the person who hurt you. It's the same amount. When you're ready, say aloud (under your breath works too): "[Name], I forgive you, in Jesus' name. I bless you to become everything your Heavenly Father created you to be. Jesus, thank You for healing my heart and helping me walk forward in freedom and peace."

STUDENT ASSIGNMENTS FOR NEXT WEEK

- Student 1: Bring a joke (< 1 min)
- Student 2: Bring a real God story (< 2 min)

👉 Student 3: Bring something kind or encouraging to share (< 2 min)

FACILITATOR NOTES ✨

Week 10

Brain Pictures: *God Uses Your Imagination*

OPENING

Open with a 1-minute prayer, inviting Holy Spirit. Take a moment to celebrate what God has done over these 10 weeks!

Student Activations

- Student 1: Appropriate Joke (< 1 min)
- Student 2: God story / Testimony (< 2 min)
- Student 3: Encouragement for the Group (< 2 min)

REVIEW: WHAT WE'VE COVERED

Take 5 minutes to let students recap anything they've found themselves using or thinking about over the past weeks. What has stuck? What has God been doing?

SCRIPTURAL FOUNDATION

"But it was to us that God revealed these things by his Spirit. For his Spirit searches out everything and shows us God's deep secrets... And we have received God's Spirit (not the world's spirit), so we can know the wonderful things God has freely given us. ... But we understand these things, for we have the mind of Christ." **— 1 Corinthians 2:10,12,16 NLT**

Write the vision clearly; make it plain to understand, so it may be advanced to others. **— Habakkuk 2:2**

YOUR IMAGINATION IS A GIFT FROM GOD

Your imagination — the pictures and ideas that come to your mind — is one of the key ways your natural self interfaces with the spiritual realm. When Jesus is your Lord and Savior and you have Holy Spirit in you, your imagination becomes a sanctified tool: something consecrated and set apart for good purposes.

It is where you get to dream with God. It's where you can picture who He made you to be, and what He's calling you toward. It's also where your faith grows — as you envision what's possible, your capacity for it expands.

Your imagination can help you:

- *Dream big with God* — picture yourself writing that book, creating that art, speaking with confidence, reaching that goal
- *Bring scripture to life* — picture the storylines as if you were there
- *Remember God's goodness* — think back on stories of His faithfulness in your life and the lives of others
- *Envision a future filled with His promises* — what does life look like when you fully trust His plan?

Your imagination is also where you do battle. With Holy Spirit in you, when the enemy tries to plant temptations or fear into your thoughts, you have the power and authority to reject those thoughts and replace them with what's true. Speak scripture and truths that align with God's ways over yourself and your situation.

GROUP DISCUSSION

💬 What is a dream or goal you carry in your heart — something you sense God has placed there?

💬 Is there a version of your future that feels too big, or that you've been afraid to let yourself imagine? What would it look like to let yourself dream with God about it?

💬 How have you seen your imagination work for you over this course — in journaling, in the listening prayer exercises, in picturing Jesus?

💡 ACTIVATION: Close your eyes. What is one dream or goal in your heart? Take a moment and imagine yourself doing it successfully — with God's help. Thank Him that it's possible. Then write it down or draw it. Next: ask Holy Spirit, "What is one practical step I can take this week to start preparing for this dream?" Write that down too.

LAUGHING AT LIES — FINAL ROUND

One more time: write a lie from the past week on the board. Laugh at it together. Replace it with truth. This is a habit we're building for life — and you're already doing it.

GROUP CONNECT & CELEBRATION

Go around the room. Each student answers one of the following:

◆ What is the most impactful thing you've learned over these 10 weeks?

◆ What is one thing God has been doing in you during this time?

◆ What is a next step you want to take in your faith journey from here?

Students: Keep going! You were truly made for this.

CLOSING PRAYER

"Thank You, Heavenly Father, for the time we've had to grow together. Come and seal in everything we've learned. Show us how to live it out. We receive Your wisdom, Your presence, and Your Spirit working in and through us. We say yes to the life You've planned for us. In Jesus' name — amen."

FACILITATOR NOTES

About the Author: My Journey

Growing spiritually—and growing in all areas of life—is exciting to me. I love learning new things, testing them out, and then sharing with others. One of the greatest blessings in this season of my life has been growing alongside my daughters and their friends and sharing what I learn with them.

Although I was raised as a Christian and have considered myself one my whole life, I haven't always lived it—especially in my teens, 20s, and even into my 30s. Many times, I tried my best to be a good person, to pray, and to read my Bible, but it seemed like something was still missing. A couple of years into the COVID pandemic, I found myself getting worse, not better as a person. I was more anxious, more fearful, and more judgmental. It didn't feel like Christianity was working for me.

That led me to three big questions:

1. Does God care about and actively work in the world today?
2. Do signs, miracles, and wonders from Bible times still happen today?
3. What is Holy Spirit's role in the Christian life?

I had read about Holy Spirit, but I didn't really understand.

A Life-Changing Journey

Those questions took me on an incredible journey, and my life hasn't been the same since. Looking back, I now see that the books, people and resources I subsequently discovered were divinely placed in my path. They answered the very questions I had been seeking, and I realized that God had been leading me all along.

✓ **Yes, God actively cares**—not just about the world as a whole, but about the big and small details of our lives. He is a good, loving Father in heaven who wants to be involved in our daily lives. His thoughts toward us are more numerous than the grains of sand on the seashore, and He is always communicating with us.

✓ **Yes, miracles still happen.** I have seen and heard signs, miracles, and wonders happening in my own life and in the lives of those around me. I believe we are living in a time when these things are increasing all over the world.

✓ **And yes, Holy Spirit is our key to living a thriving and empowered Christian life.**

The Role of Holy Spirit

I have come to understand that Holy Spirit is *the secret sauce* of living out Christianity. Being filled, baptized, and overflowing with the Holy Spirit is what empowers us to live out our faith fully. He gives us the strength to walk in freedom and boldness, the ability to influence and impact those around us, and a greater awareness of God's love and guidance. I'm also a firm believer that we should desire to bring our understanding and experiences up to that of the Bible, not bring the Bible down to our current level of experiences and understanding.

When Jesus was on earth, He told His followers that it would be *better* if He left so that they (and we!) could receive the Holy Spirit (John 16:7). That means Holy Spirit empowerment was always part of God's plan for humanity. The same Spirit that raised Christ from the dead lives in us, equipping us to do even greater things than Jesus did (John 14:12).

Encouragement for Your Journey

Wherever you are in your spiritual journey, I hope these weekly lessons encourage and inspire you. My prayer is that they are practical, easy to test and implement, and simple to share with others.

Your future is so bright. You are here on earth *on purpose and for a purpose,* created with love by a Heavenly Father who has a wonderful path laid out for you. He is so excited to walk alongside you on this adventure of life.

YouTube: @TheEncouragingMom411

Instagram: the.encouraging.mom.411

Amazon: Girls Walking With God: Growing in Faith, Identity, and Spiritual Strength [a 30-day devotional]

www.ingramcontent.com/pod-product-compliance
Lightning Source LLC
LaVergne TN
LVHW011050110826
845149LV00015B/3439

* 9 7 9 8 9 9 5 9 1 6 0 0 0 *